Copyright page and half-title page Copyright © 2020 by Humor Heals Us. All rights reserved. No part of this book may be reproduced in any form without permission in writing from the publisher. Please send bulk order requests to Humorhealsus@gmail.com Printed and bound in the USA. 978-1-63731-033-5 humorhealsus.com

Follow us on FB and IG @humorhealsus
To vote on new title names and freebies, visit us at humorhealsus.com for more information.

@humorhealsus   @humorhealsus

Farting without you is like....

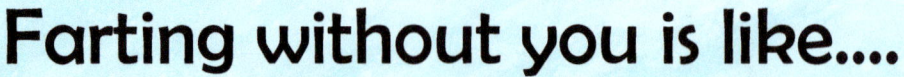

Elmer without glue

Detective without a clue

Witches without a brew

Tigger without Pooh

www.ingramcontent.com/pod-product-compliance
Lightning Source LLC
Chambersburg PA
CBHW041524070526
44585CB00002B/71